Vicar's
RELIGIOUS
JOKE BOOK

Vicar Joe's RELIGIOUS JOKE BOOK

Kevin Johns & Peter Read

y Lolfa

Illustrations: Noel Ford
Cover design: Alan Thomas

ISBN: 9781847711632

Printed on acid-free and partly recycled paper
and published and bound in Wales by
Y Lolfa Cyf., Talybont, Ceredigion SY24 5HE
e-mail ylolfa@ylolfa.com
website www.ylolfa.com
tel (01970) 832 304
fax 832 782

Contents

INTRODUCTION

For some people, religion and humour go together as easily as root canal work at the dentist's and a plateful of chocolate éclairs. Too often the church is linked with boredom and seriousness. Compiling this book, we have come to realise that lots of funny things happen in places of worship. There are so many ceremonies where something can go wrong. Total immersion is asking for trouble and this book is also brimming with stories of mayhem in christenings, weddings, Sunday services and even funerals.

The role of a clergyman or clergywoman is one of the strangest jobs on earth. Having to be holy and a shining example to the rest of the community is quite a tall order. As many of the stories prove, there is a rich vein of humour in the fact that for twenty-four hours a day, seven days a week, there are thousands of professional church people trying to be near-perfect representations of God on earth. In fairness, many of the clergy with whom we've spoken and met have been the first to tell jokes against themselves.

GK Chesterton once wrote that the test of a good religion is how much it can laugh at itself. Despite its negative perception amongst many non-attendees, the church should be a happy and jolly place. After all, when

Jesus explained the kingdom of God he often used the analogies of parties and wine. You can't get much happier than a good bottle of red!

We've had fun compiling this book. All the religious books we found seemed fairly ancient and rarely modern, so we felt it was time for a new one. We tried to resist the temptation to cram it with 'have you heard the one about…' jokes. Whilst you will find some tales of that genre, we have tried to complement them with true stories, faux pas, epitaphs and general statements made by the famous and infamous about matters of life and death.

You may already be wondering who Vicar Joe is and why this book bears his name. He was created in 2006 when Peter Read was asked to write a play about football for Swansea Grand Theatre. The comedy, which was called *Toshack or Me!* featured a vicar (Joe) who was so keen on watching Swansea City that he cancelled weddings if they clashed with matches. He also refused to marry one couple where the groom-to-be supported Swansea and she followed Cardiff City. Vicar Joe's sermons had more references to the Premiership and the League than to holy scripture and he also got into hot water for praying from the pulpit, asking the Lord to deliver his humble side against the pride of Premiership might. In 2008 Vicar Joe reappeared in the play *To Hull and Back*, whilst in February 2009 the one-man shoe *Vicar Joe* was premiered at Swansea Grand Theatre Arts

Wing. Vicar Joe is played by Kevin Johns.

We hope the book will be used to lighten up and brighten up sermons here, there and everywhere. It might also be used by after-dinner speakers or just be the means of tickling you pink whenever you read *Vicar Joe's Religious Joke Book*. It would be pleasing to think we created guffaws on British Rail, national and local bus services. Go on, give it a try. Happy reading and laughing.

Peter Read and Kevin Johns

1. THINGS PEOPLE SAY

When people in Hell irritate each other, where do they tell them to go?

*   *   *

Everybody ought to have a religion. You owe it to yourself to know what church you're staying away from.

*   *   *

One clergyman to another: "There's a lot to be said for sin. We'd be out of a job without it!"

*   *   *

An atheist is a man who goes to a Celtic versus Rangers match and doesn't care who wins.

*   *   *

An educated chimpanzee, on reading Darwin's *Origin of the Species*, said, "Goodness, I am my brother's keeper."

I know why the sun never sets on the British Empire.
God wouldn't trust an Englishman in the dark.
  – Duncan Speath

* * *

A man believed so strongly in reincarnation that he
wrote out a will leaving everything to himself.

*   *   *

A Welshman was shipwrecked at sea and marooned on a desert island. When a passing vessel picked him up five years later the crew were amazed to find his little island covered in fine buildings that he had built himself. With pride, the Welsh Robinson Crusoe took the captain round the island and pointed out to him his house, workshop, electricity generator and two chapels. "But what do you need the second chapel for?" asked the captain. "Oh, that's the one I don't go to," he replied.

*   *   *

Jesus obviously wasn't an Englishman because he never wore socks with his sandals.

*   *   *

Jesus could never have been born in Wales, as there are no wise men in the East to visit him.

*   *   *

A tribe of cannibals were converted to Christianity. Now on Fridays they only eat fishermen.

*   *   *

A short-sighted penguin escaped from the zoo, wandered into a convent by mistake and had a nervous breakdown. He thought he must have shrunk.

* * *

A good sermon should be like a woman's skirt – short enough to retain the interest but long enough to cover the essentials.

* * *

CHRISTIAN CHAT-UP LINES

Nice Bible.

I would very much like to pray with you.

You know Jesus? Me too.

God told me to talk to you.

I know a nice church where we could go and talk.

How about a hug, sister?

Do you need help carrying your Bible? It looks heavy.

Christians don't shake hands, Christians gotta hug.

Did it hurt when you fell from Heaven?

What have you got planned tonight? Fancy a Bible study?

I am here for you.

CREATION RAP

In September 2008 scientists in Switzerland began an historic Big Bang experiment, an effort to learn more about how the universe began. However, Vicar Joe was incensed when the wacky scientists – involved in an experiment which could have created a giant black hole capable of swallowing the planet – posted a rap video on YouTube. So, in protest, Vicar Joe wrote and performed a 'Creation Rap' during the Sunday Morning Service:

I created the world many years ago
I made all the colours from red to indigo
But science don't believe me, they get in such a flap
So I have written the 'Creation Rap'.
At first I made the heavens and then the earth
And then to the people I gave birth.
I planted some trees for the birds and the bees
And then to Eve I gave really great … knees.
But still they don't believe me and they created a big bang
I iz always listening but the phone it never rang.
Now they've spent 4.4 billion and the cupboard is bare,
But for the hungry and the homeless I iz always there!

2. PREACHERS AND RELIGIOUS LEADERS

A young vicar was at a civic function standing next to an older, rather miserable vicar. A waitress came to them, carrying a tray full of glasses of wine. The young vicar took one and the waitress offered the tray to the older clergyman. He put up his hand and said, "I'd sooner commit adultery than let a sip of alcohol pass my lips." The younger vicar put his glass back on the tray, smiled at the waitress and said, "I'm terribly sorry, I didn't realise there was a choice."

*   *   *

A bishop was present at a dinner party and was sitting next to the beautiful hostess. As the evening progressed he noticed that she and the rest of the company imbibed several glasses of wine, but he wasn't offered a drink. Eventually, he asked in an exasperated voice: "Do you think I could have a glass of wine?"

The hostess threw up her hands in horror: "Bishop, I'm so sorry. I thought you were president of the Temperance Society."

The bishop replied, "No, I am president of the Anti-Vice League."

"Ah," said the stunning hostess, "I knew there was something I couldn't offer you."

* * *

A church dignitary had drunk too much wine at a conference. The hotel porter took him to what he thought was his room. As the churchman staggered around the bedroom he noticed, laid out on the bed, a saucy, naughty nightdress. He lifted it, surveyed it, and then holding it aloft said to the porter, "What is this?"

"That, sir," said the porter, "is a ladies nighty."

The churchman turned to the porter and said in the best ecclesiastical voice he could muster: "Take it away and fill it for me."

* * *

The newly-ordained Catholic priests went out on the town to celibate.

* * *

Lord George Brown was a colourful member of the Labour government in the Wilson era. In addition to being a politician, he was renowned for his love and consumption of alcohol. On one occasion he was sent to Peru by the government. He spoke at a function, but had drunk a large amount of alcohol before giving his speech. At the end of the speech he sat down and promptly fell asleep.

Other people spoke while George slept. He was finally awakened by the band playing the national anthem. As he focussed his eyes, he saw people getting up from their seats and noticed a vision of beauty dressed in red, across what he assumed was the dance floor. He went over to this vision of beauty and said, "Will you do me the honour of this dance?"

The reply came: "I will not dance with you for three reasons. First, you are drunk. Secondly, it is not a dance, it is our national anthem and thirdly, I am the Cardinal of Lima."

*   *   *

Vicar Joe was at a Council of Churches service where a preacher was completing a temperance sermon, a fiery delivery about the evils of alcohol. From the high pulpit he declared with great expression: "If I had all the beer in the world, I'd take it and throw it in the river. If I had all the whisky in the world, I'd take it and throw it in the river."

Before he sat down, the preacher asked for a hymn with which to close the service.

"258," boomed Vicar Joe, "'Shall We Gather at the River?'"

＊　　＊　　＊

A vicar lost his umbrella. The verger said, "Perhaps someone from the congregation has stolen it." So the vicar and verger formed a pact that the next Sunday the vicar would preach on the Ten Commandments. When the vicar reached 'Thou Shalt Not Steal' the verger would look around the congregation to see if anyone looked uncomfortable. But, to the verger's astonishment, the vicar preached on a totally different subject and didn't mention the Ten Commandments. At the end of the service, the verger asked him why he had changed his plans.

"I'm sorry," said the vicar, "I should have told you. When I was thinking about the Ten Commandments in my study and I came to 'Thou Shalt Not Commit Adultery', I remembered where I'd left the umbrella."

＊　　＊　　＊

One Saturday evening a vicar told his wife: "I don't think the congregation listen to a word I say in my sermons. Tomorrow, I think I'll preach about riding a bike." On the Sunday morning, as he mounted the steps, he changed his mind and decided to preach about sex.

The following Tuesday, the vicar's wife, who had not been in the service, was shopping in Tesco's when a member of the congregation stopped her in the aisle and said, "Tell your husband that was the best sermon I've ever heard him preach."

"I will," said the vicar's wife, "but I must admit I'm surprised it went so well, as he's only done it twice in his life. And the second time he fell off."

*　　*　　*

During an executive meeting of the Council of Churches there was the smell of burning in the hall where the meeting was being held. The Salvation Army officer leapt to his feet, shouting, "Fire, fire!" The Presbyterian stood up and shouted, "Order, order!" The Baptist got to his feet and said excitedly, "Water, water!" The Anglican remained seated and said, "I think we should set up a sub-committee to look into the matter."

*　　*　　*

Two boys were trading insults when they were in school. In later life, one of them became a bishop and the other a colonel in the army. One day, by sheer coincidence, they found themselves dressed in full regalia, sitting on a platform seat waiting for a train. The bishop looked at the colonel and said, "Excuse me, porter, am I on the right platform for Manchester?"

"Yes, you are, madam," the colonel replied, "but should you be travelling in your condition?"

Okay, I'll admit we Christians took the ten commandments from you, but you can't accuse us of keeping them!

A Jew was arguing with a Christian: "Your whole religion is based on ours anyway. You even took the Ten Commandments from us."

"But you can't accuse us of keeping them," said the Christian.

*   *   *

A bishop was being interviewed on television on his 90th birthday. In closing, the interviewer said, "Thank you for coming, my Lord, and perhaps I may have the pleasure of interviewing you on your 100th birthday."

"No reason why not," said the bishop, "you appear to be in fairly good health."

*   *   *

Archbishop McGee had a waiter drop hot soup down his neck. The archbishop said, "Is there a layman present who will kindly express my true feelings?"

*   *   *

Archbishop Trench, throughout his life, feared paralysis. One evening he was at a function and whilst everyone was eating their food, he put down his knife and fork, looked up and said, "That's it. It's happened. I'm paralysed. I've lost all feeling in my left leg." The woman sitting next to him said, "Archbishop, you are fine. Throughout the evening it's my leg you've been pinching."

*   *   *

A bishop had a bad reputation in his diocese for preaching long and very boring sermons. His reputation spread rapidly, because each Sunday he used to visit a different parish to preach. One day he arrived at five to eleven at a small country church and was welcomed by the vicar who was looking a bit flustered. He led the bishop into the church and, to the bishop's surprise and annoyance, there were only three people in the congregation.

"Didn't you tell them I was coming?" he asked the vicar angrily.

"I certainly did not, Bishop," replied the vicar, "but I shall find out who did."

* * *

A vicar prided himself on his spontaneity. He told his friend that he was able to preach a sermon on any subject at a moment's notice. His friend challenged him to do so the following Sunday and said he would put a piece of paper with the required subject in the pulpit, just before the service.

When the time for the sermon came, the clergyman mounted the pulpit and found the slip of paper. It said "constipation". Opening the Bible, the vicar said, "My text, this morning, is taken from the book of Exodus, chapter 34: 'And Moses took the tablets and went into the mountain.'"

* * *

The vicar's wife said to the visitor at the door:
"I'm afraid the vicar is out, but if it's really important, he will see you."

*   *   *

"I shall omit the blessing this Sunday," said the minister, "I don't think you need it. The Lord said 'Blessed are the poor', and judging by the size of the collection, that covers you all."

*   *   *

In the confession box the young girl said to the priest: "Father, I have to admit I spend an awful lot of time looking at myself in the mirror and saying, 'Gillian, you are beautiful.' Is that a sin of pride, Father?"

"No," replied the priest, after looking at her carefully, "just a mistake."

*   *   *

In a cricket match between two teams of clergy, the local bishop opened the innings. A young curate was the opening bowler and in deference to the bishop's office sent up a slow half-volley with the intention of helping the portly bishop to 'get off the mark'. The bishop struck the ball out of the ground. He turned to the curate and said, "I'm sorry, young man, but I seem to have hit you out of your parish." The curate smiled, and feeling slightly peeved, walked slowly back to his mark. He turned, ran in and sent in a vicious bouncer. This hit the bishop in the midriff and he collapsed to the ground in agony. The young curate rushed up to him and said, "I'm sorry, m'lord, but I seem to have hit you in the middle of your diocese."

*　　*　　*

Nuns in a convent called one of their number who had a wooden leg, 'Hopalong Chastity'.

*　　*　　*

At an ecclesiastical conference, a reporter came into the dining room for breakfast. It was a freezing December morning, and all the clergymen were gathered around the blazing log fire. The journalist sat alone at a table, shivering. He suddenly said: "I dreamt I'd ended up in Hell last night." Most of them ignored him, but one cleric said: "Really, what was it like?"

"Not all that different from now," the journalist replied. "You couldn't get near the fire for clergymen."

*　　*　　*

Vicar Joe had married a couple. In the vestibule the groom apologised and said that he had no money to pay for the service, as he had been under the impression it was free. "I tell you what," said Vicar Joe, "just give me what you think the bride is worth." The groom went into his pocket and gave him a tenner. Vicar Joe took the money, looked closely at the bride, then gave the groom £5 change.

3. PITY ABOUT THE CONGREGATION

"I hear she had her husband cremated. Isn't that typical! Some of us can't get a husband for love nor money – others have husbands to burn."

*   *   *

"Your husband walked out in the middle of my sermon last Sunday, Mrs Jones."

"It was nothing personal, Vicar, he was just sleepwalking."

*   *   *

"Do you go to church on a Sunday morning or do you sleep late?"

"Both."

*   *   *

Anglican congregations often begin their service with the vicar saying: "The Lord be with you," to which they reply: "And also with you." One Sunday morning the vicar said, "I think there is something wrong with the mike." There wasn't, and the congregation replied: "And also with you."

*   *   *

One Sunday a minister told his congregation that the church needed some extra money and asked the people to prayerfully consider giving a little extra in the collection plate. He said that whoever gave the most would be able to pick out three hymns.

After the offering plates were passed, the pastor glanced down and noticed that someone had placed £200 in the collection. He was so excited that he immediately shared his joy with the congregation and said he'd like to personally thank the person who had placed the money on the plate.

A lady sitting at the back shyly raised her hand. The vicar asked her to come to the front and told her how wonderful it was that she gave so much and in thanksgiving asked her to pick out three hymns.

Her eyes brightened as she looked over the congregation, pointed to the three most handsome men in the building and said: "I'll take him and him and him!"

*   *   *

The following sermon was preached in the parish church on Stir-up Sunday in 1973. It was preached in response to a chorister's remark: "The preachers in this church have nothing to say and take an age to say it."

The sermon:

Preachers are often accused of being long-winded. Indeed, on one occasion, much to the annoyance of the vicar, I myself preached for three-quarters of an hour. But not this morning! This morning, I intend to take the advice of Richard Baxter and preach as a dying man to dying men, and simply say today is Stir-up Sunday, and if in the next twelve months we don't stir ourselves and do something about the many problems that confront us as a parish, *then*, God help us!

In the stunned silence that followed, an elderly parishioner was heard to remark: "What did he say?"

*   *   *

Many people have nothing but praise for the church – especially when the collection plate is passed around.

*   *   *

Three Scotsmen attended church. When the collection plate arrived at their pew, one fainted and the other two carried him out.

*   *   *

"Remember, my friends," said the vicar, summing up a sermon on the dangers of drinking and driving, "whisky and petrol don't mix."

"They do," said someone knowingly in the back of the church, "but it tastes terrible!"

*   *   *

A priest announced one Sunday that his sermon the following week would be on the topic of lying. As preparation, he asked all the members of the congregation to read Genesis chapter 51. The following week he began his sermon by asking all those who hadn't read the chapter to put up their hands. There was no response and so he began by saying: "In that case, the sermon on the theme of lying should be quite appropriate as there are only 50 chapters in Genesis."

*   *   *

Shaking hands with his congregation after the service, the vicar was delighted when the parishioner commented that his sermon had been like the peace and mercy of God. The vicar wasn't so impressed when, reading his Concordance, he saw the words: "The peace of God passes all understanding and his mercy endures for ever."

*   *   *

A retired minister was asked to preach in a church in place of the booked preacher who was taken ill. He began his sermon by pointing to a window in the church which was broken and had been covered with hardboard. "I feel a little like that piece of hardboard," he said, "I'm not the real thing. I'm like a substitute for that glass."

His sermon went on, and on, and on, until he finally drew to a close after sixty-five minutes of speaking. On the door, one member of the congregation shook his hand and said: "You shouldn't do yourself down and say you're just a substitute. You were a real pain (pane)."

*   *   *

When few people had personal transport, it was the usual practice of remote chapels to offer the visiting preachers both morning and evening services, with meals provided in between.

In this particular isolated chapel, in Yorkshire, the visiting preacher had duly taken the morning service and then enjoyed a sumptuous lunch provided by local steward, Fred, and his wife Gladys. At teatime, after a rest, he was offered the usual substantial tea, but declined this, declaring that he never took a big meal immediately before a service as his preaching seemed to suffer.

Thus, after just a cup of tea, he preached again at the

evening service, and afterwards, saying his farewells, he asked Fred and Gladys what they thought of his sermon.

"Well," said Gladys, "tha might as well 'ave 'ad thee tea, Lad!"

* * *

The ladies praise the curate's eyes –
I never see their light divine;
For when he prays he closes his,
And when he preaches closes mine.

* * *

"I intend to put together a volume of my sermons to be published posthumously."
"I really look forward to that."

* * *

Many preachers think of the back row in their church as the Bermuda triangle – where everything they say, sinks without trace.

* * *

Sunday School teacher: "Suppose we want to pray to God for forgiveness. What must we do first of all?"
Small boy: "Sin."

* * *

The congregation were struggling to hear what the vicar was saying because of a crying baby. The baby's mother got up to leave.

"It's quite alright," said the vicar, "he's not disturbing me."

"Maybe not, but you're disturbing him," said the mother.

* * *

A fella was coming out of church one day, and the vicar was standing at the door as always to shake hands. He grabbed the man by the hand and pulled him aside. The vicar said to him: "You need to join the Army of the Lord."

The man replied: "I'm already in the Army of the Lord, Reverend."

The vicar questioned: "How come I don't see you except at Christmas and Easter?"

He whispered back, "I'm in the secret service."

* * *

"Your suit will be ready in three months, sir."

"Three months! It only took six days to make the world."

"Yes – and have you seen the state it's in?"

*　　*　　*

A parson walking through the village saw a well-known prostitute walking towards him. "I prayed for you last night," he said in a disapproving tone.

"Silly," she said, "you should have rung me. I was free all night."

*　　*　　*

The Dean of Enniskillen visited an elderly lady in the parish. She confided that she believed her maid was plotting to get her hands on her money, because every time she went near the maid's parrot, the creature would screech: "I wish the old lady were dead." The dean told her that he too had a parrot, which he had trained to recite the litany. He suggested they put the two parrots together so that the dean's could influence the maid's bird. This was done, and the next time the lady of the manor approached them, the maid's parrot screeched, "I wish the old lady were dead," and the dean's parrot replied: "We beseech thee to hear us, good Lord."

*　　*　　*

"Vicar Joe," said the sick old lady, "I have two final requests. First, I want to be cremated, and secondly, I want my ashes scattered all over the Liberty Stadium."

"Why the Liberty?" asked Vicar Joe. "You hate football."

"I do, but at least I'll be sure my children visit me once a fortnight during the season."

*   *   *

Vicar Joe was visiting the homes of his parishioners. At one house it seemed obvious that someone was at home, but no answer came to his repeated knocks on the door. Therefore, he took out a card and wrote: "Revelation 3:20" ("Behold I stand at the door and knock") on the back of it and stuck it in the door.

When the offering was processed the following Sunday, he found that his card had been returned. Added to it was this cryptic message: "Genesis 3:10." Reaching for his Bible to check out the citation, Joe broke up into gales of laughter. Genesis 3:10 reads: "I heard your voice in the garden and I was afraid, for I was naked."

*   *   *

Stan Ford was a well-known evangelist from Merseyside. He was a strong, well-built man and before his conversion to Christianity had been a heavyweight boxing champion. On one occasion he was preaching in the open air at Pier Head in Liverpool. A man in the audience kept heckling and interrupting Stan. Eventually,

Stan stopped speaking, came down off his soap box, knelt on the ground and in a position of prayer looked up to Heaven and said: "Lord, would it be possible to have five minutes off, so I can sort this bloke out?" As Stan rose, the heckler fled.

*　　*　　*

Donald Soper was speaking in Tower Hill one lunch-time when a heckler shouted out: "Christianity's been around for two thousand years and look at the state of the world."

Soper replied: "Soap's been around for ages, and look at the state of your neck."

*　　*　　*

A man on a train found himself sitting between a rabbi and a priest. "Ah, the Old and the New Testament," he said, laughing. "Yes," said the priest, "and the space between them is normally completely blank."

*　　*　　*

One Saturday night, a girl 'sowed her wild oats' and then on Sunday morning went to church to pray for a crop failure.

*　　*　　*

A tourist visiting the Holy Land went to the Sea of Galilee to see the place where Jesus walked on water. He thought he would take a boat ride across the lake but on being told it would cost £15 he declined. He told the boat owner: "I'm not surprised Jesus walked, at those prices."

* * *

An Irishman was smuggling a large bottle of whisky across the border between Eire and Northern Ireland. The customs officer asked him what was in the bottle.

"Holy water," said the Irishman.

The customs officer insisted on opening the bottle and when he took a whiff he said: "This is whisky."

The Irishman said: "Saints be praised, it's a miracle."

*   *   *

Martha Irving, a housewife from Southwell, Notts, put her handbag down on a charity stall during a Methodist jumble sale in August 1983. It contained £155 in cash. When she returned a few seconds later, the handbag had been sold for 20 pence.

*   *   *

Three vicars from St David's diocese were having lunch together.

One said: "Duw, since summer started I've been having trouble with bats in my loft and attic at church. I've tried everything – noise, sprays, cats – nothing seems to scare them away."

Another said: "Yeah, me too. I've got hundreds living in the bell tower and in the roof of the vicarage. I've even had the place fumigated, and they won't go away."

The third said: "I've had the same problem. I made them members of the church … haven't seen one back since!"

*   *   *

In the early 1950s the quiet life of our small suburban village was changed. We were engulfed by a new housing development. We lost our status as a conventional district and became a new parish. We built a new church, and our old dual-purpose building became the church hall. Our old priest-in-charge now became the vicar of the new parish, and called a meeting of the PCC to consider the use and renting of the church hall. He opened the meeting by saying that, as a new Church of England parish, we were responsible for the interests of everyone living in the parish, so the hall should be available to all-comers at a reasonable charge. To which an irate church warden responded: "Vicar, what do you think the church is? A charitable organisation?"

* * *

A fierce principal of a theological college was addressing the new students. He told the male students: "If I catch any of you in a female room after eleven o'clock at night I'll fine you £5. If I catch you a second time I'll fine you £10. If I see you there a third time, you'll pay a £20 fine."

Suddenly, one of the new male students put up his hand.

"Yes?" barked the principal.

"Please could you tell me how much a season ticket costs?"

An atheist was climbing up a rock face and realised he was in danger of falling. He clutched a bush, but knew that it was only a matter of time before he would have to let go. He shouted at the top of his voice: "Please help me. Is anyone there?"

A voice responded, "Let go. This is God. I will catch you."

There was a long pause and then the man said, "Excuse me. Is anyone else there, please?"

*   *   *

A lady, whose husband had been a waiter at a large restaurant, attended a séance after his death. She suddenly felt a message coming through from the other side. "Jack, Jack, is that you?" she shouted. "Speak to me. Come to me, Jack."

The voice came back: "I can't, it's not my table."

4. CHILDREN'S TAKE
ON RELIGION

A bishop, dressed in all his regalia, was visiting a primary school. "I'll give 5p to the first boy or girl who can tell me who I am."

A small boy put up his hand and said: "Please sir, you are God."

"No, I'm not," said the bishop, "but here's 20p."

*   *   *

A nother bishop was presenting the prizes at a school. He got tired of saying the same words of congratulations to every pupil. When a pretty blonde girl came up for her prize, he thought he would try something different. He shook her hand and asked: "What are you going to do when you leave school?" Blushing, the girl replied, "Well, Bishop, I was going to go home for tea. But I could change that, if you like."

*   *   *

T he primary school children were excited because the Archbishop was visiting them. The head teacher spent a long time preparing them for the big day. She explained to them that he was a very important man, and if he addressed them they must reply: "My Lord."

When he arrived, he singled out a six-year-old boy and, smiling at him, asked: "How old are you?" Confused and overawed, the little boy gasped: "My God, I'm six!"

*   *   *

Billy Graham tells a story about getting lost while looking for the post office in a small town where he was due to speak. Eventually, a young boy gave him a ride on the back of his bike. Billy Graham thanked him and told him to bring his family that evening to hear his sermon. "I will tell you how to get to Heaven," he told the boy. The boy looked at him derisively. "I don't think so. You don't even know the way to the post office."

*   *   *

While questioning young children at a confirmation service, Vicar Joe asked: "Who is it that sees all and knows all, and before whom, even I am a mere worm?"

A small girl answered: "Please sir, my mam."

*   *   *

Sunday School teacher: "When boys and girls do naughty things, do you know where they go?"

Small boy: "To the sand dunes, if the weather's fine."

*   *   *

A Sunday School teacher had just finished describing the delights of Heaven. "Hands up all those who'd like to go to Heaven?" All the children put up their hands except one little boy. "Don't you want to go to Heaven, Billy?"

"I can't, Miss," he replied tearfully, "my mum told me to come straight home."

*   *   *

Her two sons were kneeling on the ground with their hands together, and five-year-old Tommy was saying grace.

"What are you doing?" asked their mother. "You only say grace when you're having a meal."

Tommy pointed to his younger brother. "I know. He's just swallowed a worm."

*   *   *

Two young children were watching their grand-mother reading the Good Book. "Why does Gran spend so much time reading the Bible?"

"I think she's studying for her final exams."

*   *   *

A Catholic family and a Protestant family went on holiday together to the South of France. As the beach was secluded and the weather warm, they allowed the Catholic boy and the Protestant girl to go swimming without any costumes. When they came out of the water, the little boy was beaming and said: "We've had a lovely time, and now we know the difference between Catholics and Protestants."

*   *   *

A Sunday School teacher began her lesson with the question: "Boys and girls, what do we know about God?"

A hand shot up in the air: "He's an artist."

"Really? How do you know that?" asked the teacher.

"You know… Our Father, who does art in Heaven…"

*   *   *

In Yorkshire, the Sunday School nativity play was going well until Wise Man Number One forgot his lines:
WISE MAN: … (silence)

PROMPTER (whispering): I bring you a gift of gold.
STILL SILENCE
PROMPTER (whispering): I bring you a gift of gold.
MORE SILENCE
PROMPTER (louder whisper): Well – say something!
WISE MAN (studying the crib): Ee… int 'e like 'is dad!

*   *   *

PARSON (from the pulpit): We will now sing hymn number two hundred and twenty two; two, two, two; 'Ten Thousand times Ten Thousand'; two, two, two.

WORRIED BOY IN PEW, TO HIS FATHER: Do we 'ave to work it out, dad?

*   *   *

A little boy returning home from his first service asked his mother what the preacher had meant when he said "dust to dust, ashes to ashes". His mother replied: "It means we all come from dust and we shall all return to dust."

That night, the little boy shouted from his bedroom: "Come quickly, Mummy, there's someone under the bed, either coming or going."

*   *   *

A girl opened the family Bible. She stared in awe at the large pressed leaf lying between the first two pages. "Look," she said, "it's Adam's suit."

* * *

The vicar's wife was entertaining some small children to tea. Turning to one young girl, she said, "I understand God has sent you a little brother."

"Yes. And He knows where the extra money is coming from to feed him. I heard Daddy tell Mummy."

* * *

It was Mark's first visit to Sunday School. At the end the teacher said: "Now children, let's kneel and say our prayers."

Mark said, "I can't. I haven't brought my pyjamas."

* * *

SOME CHILDREN'S PRAYERS

DISC JOCKEY'S SON: That's the end of my prayers for tonight. Tune in again on this wavelength at the same time tomorrow.

* * *

A child finished his prayers one night with the words: "And I'm afraid this is goodbye, God – tomorrow we're moving to Liverpool."

* * *

A little boy was being tucked into bed by his mother. They said prayers together and he ended: "Please bless Mummy, Daddy, and Grandma and goodbye Granddad." The mother thought it was a strange request and was even more concerned when Granddad died the next morning.

The next night, the little boy ended his prayers with: "Please bless Mummy, Daddy and goodbye Grandma." The following morning Grandma died.

On the third night, the boy concluded his prayers with: "Please bless Mummy and goodbye Daddy."

The wife thought she should tell her husband. He was beside himself with fear and the next day drove to work at about ten miles an hour. He was extremely cautious in work, standing against walls so nothing could fall on him and checking, then re-checking every chair before he sat down. After work, he drove home, once again extremely slowly and cautiously to avoid accidents.

He arrived home very late. His wife was annoyed.

"Where have you been?" she shouted.

"Don't have a go at me," he replied, "I've had an awful day."

"You've had a bad day?" she said. "It can't be any worse than mine. After you left for work today, I went downstairs, opened the door and found the milkman dead on the doorstep."

*　　*　　*

Heavenly Father bless us
And keep us all alive
There's ten of us for dinner
And not enough for five.

THE STUDENT'S PRAYER BEFORE AN EXAM

Now I lay me down to rest
And hope to pass tomorrow's test.
If I die before I wake
That's one less test I have to take.

*   *   *

"Why did Mary and Joseph take the infant Jesus to Jerusalem with them?" asked the Sunday School teacher.

"Was it because they couldn't get a babysitter?"

*   *   *

"Why did the Children of Israel make a golden calf?" asked the Sunday School teacher.

"Was it because they didn't have enough money to make a cow?"

*   *   *

"Did Moses ever get better?" the girl asked her R.E. teacher.

"He was never ill."

"Well, why did God give him so many tablets?"

*   *   *

"What did the Sunday School teacher tell you today?"

"She told us how the Children of Israel were running away from the Egyptians and when they came to the Red Sea, Moses got to build a large bridge, and when the Egyptians rushed in, the Children of Israel blew up the bridge, and…"

"The Sunday School teacher told you that?"

"No. But if I told you what she really told us, you wouldn't believe a word."

*   *   *

A girl explaining what she had learnt in Sunday School to her mother: "I heard a lovely story about a man called Adam and a woman called Eve, who were really happy until the servant came."

*   *   *

"What do you know about Elijah?" the R.E. teacher asked the class.

"Not much miss," replied a pupil, "except that he went on a cruise with a widow."

*   *   *

A little girl was talking to her teacher about whales. The teacher said it was physically impossible for a whale to swallow a human because even though it was a large mammal its throat was very small. The little girl stated that Jonah had been swallowed by a whale. Irritated, the teacher reiterated that a whale could not swallow a human; it was physically impossible.

The little girl said: "When I get to Heaven I will ask Jonah."

The teacher asked: "What if Jonah went to Hell?"

"Then you can ask him," the girl replied.

*   *   *

A boy was taken by his mother to a séance. The medium asked him if there was anyone he would like to speak to.

"My grandpa," he said.

The medium went into a trance and said in a suitably spooky voice: "This is Grandpa speaking to you from Heaven. What is it you would like to know?"

"What are you doing up there?" asked the boy. "You're not even dead yet."

5. FAUX PAS

A British preacher went over to America to speak in the various Southern Baptist churches. The Southern Baptists have a reputation for being fairly serious and unfortunately the British preacher was not aware that in America 'butt' means backside or bottom. He stood up to give his first sermon, and said: "I want to speak to you today about the Christian but," meaning that many Christians allow obstacles and difficulties to get in the way of achieving what they set out to do. "I have three points," he said. "First, every Christian has a but. Secondly, my but will be different to your but. And thirdly, in the bonds of Christian fellowship, we must learn to share each other's buts."

* * *

When Lord Fisher arrived in the United States, the journalists converged on him with a barrage of questions. One of them asked him: "Will you be visiting any nightclubs while you are in New York?"

The bishop sarcastically replied: "Are there any nightclubs in New York?"

The next day, the headline in the newspapers read: "Bishop's first question: are there any nightclubs in New York?"

*　*　*

A very popular minister was sent by his congregation for a sabbatical to Tyndale House in Cambridge. The minister was very effective in his community but was not terribly well read or educated. At breakfast, on the first morning, the warden of the college was pouring him a cup of tea. Holding the teapot in one hand and the milk jug in the other, he asked his guest: "Are you pre lactarian or post lactarian?" – meaning do you want your milk first or second. The minister didn't have a clue what the warden meant. He thought for a moment and said: "Actually, I'm a Baptist."

*　*　*

Outside a Christadelphian church they always advertised the title of the forthcoming lecture about an aspect of faith. One week, the board read: "When will Jesus Christ come again? This Sunday, 6.30pm, God willing."

*　*　*

A vicar prepared the service sheet for his own induction. Prominent on the front page was the name of the church written thus: "St Mary the Virgin? Weldon." Not a time to question the virgin birth, we're sure you will agree.

*　　*　　*

Later on in his ministry, the vicar announced in the parish magazine that "the May Queen would be drowned on the village green" at the village school May Day festivities. The young lady in question survived the ordeal unscathed.

*　　*　　*

Reg Bryant, a Swansea-based evangelist, was once on a speaking tour of North Wales. He asked the pianist at a gospel hall to play a hymn which was not in the hymn book. He hummed the tune for her.

"I'm very sorry, but I can't play by ear," she said.

"Well," he said, "why don't you move the piano over by there then?"

*　　*　　*

Whilst giving the church notices during the morning service to a packed church, the church secretary was afraid that very few would come for the evening service when they would be addressed by Linda Belch, a missionary whom the church supported. "So I implore you all," he beamed, "to come and hear Linda Belch all the way from Africa."

*　　*　　*

The omission of commas on the order of service meant that worshippers at a cathedral were informed that the anthems to be sung at Matins and Evensong would be: 'Wash Me Wesley' and 'I will wash Hopkins'.

* * *

Preachers often have too much material for a sermon. One parson began: "My dear friends, I feel somewhat like a mosquito in a nudist camp – there's so much to do, I don't know where to begin."

* * *

A South Walian lay preacher was speaking in a very posh, well-heeled church. He was known for his innovative language, dropping his aitches and putting the aitch in the wrong place. Talking about the disciples on the road to Emmaus, who were joined by the risen Christ, he described their doubts before Christ appeared in these terms: "They were 'aving it to go on the road to Hemmaus, before the risen Lord happeared to them."

* * *

The Bishop of Kensington reduced a congregation at Wormwood Scrubs to gales of laughter when he began his sermon with the words: "Peter was a man who had real convictions."

*   *   *

The minister of a large church decided to rest the elderly secretary from his weekly notice giving, which was always long and turgid. Instead, he decided to have a session where anyone could stand up and give a notice. A lady stood up and said: "I've been in this church for thirty years and it's lovely to see all the young families joining us. But every Thursday I am in the church on my own, cleaning the pews and the brasses. I put it to you young ladies that you should come and help me on a Thursday. The Lord Jesus is looking for scrubbers."

*   *   *

Letter from a church organist to the vicar: "I am sorry to say that my wife died last night. Could you please find a substitute for me for the next few weeks?"

*   *   *

A church in a Herefordshire village had the custom of the parish clerk giving out the hymn and reading the first line. One hymn began: "Hail! Thou source of every blessing." The clerk was known for being fond of alcohol. He read the first line as: "Ale! Thou source of every blessing."

*   *   *

A lady told the verger before the evening service that she had left her watch in the church after the morning service. He said he would find it for her. The verger and the lady worshipper were perplexed and worried when the vicar announced the next hymn: "Lord, her watch Thy church is keeping."

*　　*　　*

At the end of a week-long Baptist conference in Leicester, the organiser was giving votes of thanks. Before every session, Derek Moon had played the electric organ as people took to their seats. "Finally," he said, "I would like to thank the Reverend Derek Moon for his amazing organ."

*　　*　　*

An elderly preacher was speaking on the verse from the Psalms: "As pants the heart for the living waters, so pants my heart O Lord for thee." He realised that there were lots of young people in the congregation and so he leaned over the pulpit and, pointing at the young men in the back of the church, he shouted: "You see, it's your pants the Lord wants."

*　　*　　*

Mr Humphries left the high church where there was a lot of incense and went to the low church instead. He told his new vicar: "I left that other place because there was too much incest every Sunday morning and it got to my chest."

6. SPOONERISMS

When Reverend Dr Spooner was asked if he'd actually made any spoonerisms, he replied: "It's a lase bibel."

*   *   *

Spooner once said: "I'm afraid, Mr Smith, I have already detected some prowlers in your hose."

*   *   *

Addressing a hall full of young farmers, Spooner said, "It is lovely to see a hall full of tons of soil."

*   *   *

Not only did Spooner make up (or foul up) spooner-isms verbally, he acted them too. On one occasion he was accompanied by his wife when he went to catch a train. Solemnly kissing the porter goodbye for carrying his bags, he then gave his wife a tip.

*   *   *

This is the British Broadcorping Castration.

* * *

A dyslexic Satanist sold his soul to Santa.

* * *

Ladies and gentlemen, Mr Eddie Playbody will now pee for you.

* * *

You are now going to hear the bum of the flightelbee.

* * *

Stay tuned for Charles Dickens' classic, *A Sale of Two Titties*.

* * *

7. HATCH, MATCH AND DISPATCH

BAPTISM

"Name this child!" barked the scary priest.
      "Luthy, thir," lisped the terrified mother.
"Lucifer!" roared the priest." Certainly not. I baptise thee John."

*   *   *

Conscientious parents practised on their baby with a watering can for two weeks before it was baptised.

*   *   *

A tiny country Baptist chapel in Herefordshire was having its first adult baptism for many years. The minister and a helper arrived in good time to check that everything was ready for the service. When they felt the water, they realised it would be too hot for the minister and candidate to bear. The pool had been filled by two hosepipes from a water supply that was outside the building. They reconnected the hosepipes and placed them in the water, then went outside to turn on the taps. Unfortunately, the taps were extremely tight and the two men battled to release them. They spent several minutes sweating over the job in hand. Meanwhile, the little chapel was filling up. One member of the congregation couldn't understand why the hosepipes were still in the water when the baptistry was obviously full, so he took them out and placed them neatly on top of the front pew. Outside, the two men huffed and puffed and eventually released the taps. At the point of release, everybody inside the chapel was almost drowned by the sudden rush of water coming out of the strategically positioned hosepipes.

*   *   *

At a Welsh Baptist chapel in Cefn Mawr near Wrexham, the church was packed for the baptism by immersion of several young people. The baptistry was open ready for the service and the congregation sang the opening hymn with heartfelt gusto. Despite the wonderful atmosphere, Mr Davies, a deacon who was a stickler for everything being just right, noticed that the hymn board was not straight. Throughout the hymn he looked around the church agitatedly to see if anyone else had noticed the problem. No one seemed worried in the slightest. Mr Davies reached the point where he could bear it no longer, put down his hymn book and strode to the front. To reach the hymn board he had to walk around the baptistry and climb a couple of steps which led on to the pulpit. He reached up for the board and adjusted it, stepped back to check it was straight and fell into the baptistry pool.

*   *   *

At Middleton Parish church the priest noticed during the christening of a baby girl that there was no godfather standing nearby.

"Who's the godfather?" he asked.

The mother blushed and there was a long silence as members of the family looked and whispered to each other.

In the end, the grandmother leaned over the font and looking the vicar in the eye, she said: "If you knew the trouble we had getting the name of the father you wouldn't be bothered about the name of the godfather."

MARRIAGE

Much-married film star to short-sighted minister trying to find the right place in his book: "Page 37, darling – take it from the top."

*　　*　　*

"Vicar, I believe the Bible says it's wrong to profit from other people's mistakes?"

"That is correct, yes."

"In that case, how about returning the £80 I paid you for marrying me last year?"

*　　*　　*

A sailor on leave went with his girlfriend to the local padre.

"Can you marry us?" he asked.

"Well, we have to allow three weeks before…"

"Three weeks! But I've only got a 36-hour pass!"

Then, taking the minister to one side, he said, "You couldn't just say a few words to see us over the weekend?"

*   *   *

"I understand your wife converted you to Christianity."

"Absolutely. I didn't believe in Hell until I married her."

*   *   *

"My wife's an angel."

"Lucky you. Mine's still alive."

*   *   *

Two bishops were in London to attend a week's synod at Church House. They were having tea and crumpets in front of the Athenaeum, discussing how they were going to deal with the subject of the next day's conference. It was an awkward topic for a bishop – pre-marital sex.

"For instance," said one bishop, "I never slept with my wife before I married her. Did you?"

"I don't know," said the other bishop. "What was her maiden name?"

*   *   *

FUNERALS

An Irishman on his deathbed was asked by the priest if he renounced the devil. "Just a moment now, Father," he replied, "I don't think this is a good time to be making enemies."

*　　*　　*

Dave the South Walian undertaker was asked to drive up to the north of Scotland to collect the body of a Welshman who had always stipulated he wanted to be buried in his birthplace of Gwent. Realising it was going to be a long journey, he enlisted the support of his friend Charlie and they agreed to share the driving. Charlie drove up the motorway and once they started driving through towns, Dave took over. Charlie started yawning and Dave suggested he have a kip. Charlie was a big man and found it difficult to curl up in the front seat and get comfortable. Dave pulled into a lay-by and told Charlie to get in the back of the hearse and have a sleep in the empty coffin. Charlie took his friend's advice and was soon fast asleep. While Dave was driving through Perth, Charlie sat up in the coffin. He rubbed his eyes, stretched and yawned. A woman driving behind the hearse mounted the kerb and crashed through the front window of a shop. The trip turned out to be extremely expensive as Dave had to foot the bill for a new shop window and extensive repairs to the lady's car.

*   *   *

A clergyman turned up at a crematorium in Cwmbran to scatter the ashes of a member in the Garden of Rest. When he arrived at the office he was surprised to see that the urn was screwed down and did not have a removable lid. He mentioned this to the person in charge, who pointed to a young man in the office and said that Gary would accompany the clergyman into the garden. The clergyman noticed a large screwdriver sticking out of Gary's pocket. He argued that it would not be very professional for Gary to start undoing the top in the middle of the committal service. "It's OK, Reverend, I'll screw sensitively," replied Gary.

*   *   *

A vicar in Leicestershire was called at very short notice to take a service at the crematorium, as the officiant who had been booked had phoned to say he was ill. The vicar drove furiously and arrived to see the mourners assembling, ready to enter the church. Having only spoken to the crematorium manager on the phone, he knew only that the name of the deceased was Lesley. In the rush he'd forgotten to asking whether he was burying a male or a female. He parked his car and quickly moved to the front of the procession as it was time for the service. He decided to turn to the nearest mourner and ask for help.

'Father, mother, sister or brother' would describe the sex of the person he was cremating.

"I'm so sorry," he said to the mourner, "what relation was Lesley to you?"

"Cousin," came the reply.

* * *

They say such lovely things about people at their funerals, it's a shame I'm going to miss mine by just a few days.
– Bob Monkhouse

* * *

I used to hate weddings – all those old dears poking me in the stomach and saying "you're next". But they stopped all that when I started doing the same to them at funerals.
– Gail Flynn

* * *

In Liverpool, the difference between a funeral and a wedding is one less drunk.
– Paul O'Grady

* * *

A stooped old man stood, deep in thought, watching the funeral procession pass by. I whispered to him: "Who died?" He said: "The one in the first car." – Seamus Flynn

*   *   *

The family of a man who had died in Derbyshire asked for him to be buried in his favourite village, which was Brockweir in the Wye Valley. It was arranged that the internment would take place at 12 noon. Heavy snow fell on the day and the family were delayed by weather conditions. The undertakers and the minister arrived at 11.30. They eventually received a message telling them the difficulties being faced by the hearse driver and the mourners. It was also snowing heavily in Brockweir and so they decided to keep warm in a pub which had a roaring fire.

When they finally assembled at the gates of the church at 4 pm for the service, the minister led the procession, reading words from the Book of Revelation. It was quite a long walk from the gates to the door of the church, through a field now covered in several inches of snow. As he affirmed that Jesus was the resurrection and the life, the minister turned around to see if everyone was keeping up with him. As he looked back, he saw squiggly lines in the snow where the undertakers, under the influence of four hours of sitting in a warm pub, had tried desperately to walk a straight line. To his amusement, the minister realised that the sober mourners were following the trail blazed by the undertakers.

8. PREPARING FOR THE FINAL JOURNEY – DEATH

I intend to live forever. So far, so good.
  – Steve Wright

*   *   *

My old mam read the obituary column every day but she could never understand how people always die in alphabetical order.
  – Frank Carson

*   *   *

I have never killed a man, but I have read many obituaries with great pleasure.
  – Clarence Darrow

*   *   *

It seems like the only two times they pronounce you anything in life is when they pronounce you 'man and wife' or 'dead on arrival'.
  – Dennis Miller.

* * *

I don't mind dying. Trouble is, you feel so stiff the next day.
   – George Axelrod

* * *

How would you like to die?
      At the end of a sentence.
– Peter Ustinov and interviewer.

* * *

I'm dying, but otherwise I'm in very good health.
   – Dame Edith Evans

* * *

The man who invented the hokey cokey has died. His funeral was a strange affair. First they put his left leg in...
   – Al Ferrara

* * *

Martin Levine has passed away at the age of 75. Mr Levine had owned a movie theatre chain in New

York. The funeral will be held on Thursday at 2.15, 4.20, 6.30, 8.40 and 10.50.

– David Letterman

* * *

The head of Corus steel company died and went up to the pearly gates. St Peter met him and said: "I'm not sure you can come in here. You've caused so much heartache and despair with all the people you've made redundant. I think you should go to the other place." So St Peter sent him down to Hell.

A few days later the Devil was banging on the gates and he said to St Peter: "I think you should have that Corus guy in Heaven."

"Oh no," said Peter, "he's definitely one of yours."

"The trouble is, he's only been in Hell for four days and he's already closed down seven furnaces."

9. GOODBYE TO ALL THAT ... EPITAPHS AND FAREWELLS

An epitaph is a belated advertisement for a line of goods that has been permanently discontinued.
– Irvin S Cobb (1876-1944)

APPROPRIATE INSCRIPTIONS SEEN ON TOMBSTONES:

A hippie: Don't dig me, man, I'm real gone.

A waiter: God caught his eye at last.

A pin-ball addict: Please don't tilt.

A cowboy: He called Billy the Kid a coward.

An old maid: And they say you can't take it with you.

A lawyer: The prosecution rests.

A gentleman: Excuse me for not rising.

A husband (from his wife): Rest in peace Until we meet again.

*   *   *

Here lies James Woodhen
The greatest among men.

Reader, please note, his name was Woodcock, but it would not rhyme.

*   *   *

Here lives Major James Bush
Killed by the accidental discharge of his orderly's gun.
Well done, thou good and faithful servant.

*   *   *

A zealous locksmith died of late,
And did arrive at heaven's gate.
He stood without and would not knock,
Because he meant to pick the lock.
– Anonymous (1623)

*   *   *

Alack, and well a day,
Potter himself is turned to clay.
(On Archbishop Potter, 1747)

*   *   *

When I am dead, I hope it will be said:
His sins are scarlet but his books are read.
– Hilaire Belloc (1870-1953)

*   *   *

Here lies my wife: here let her lie!
Now she's at rest and so am I.
– John Dryden (1631-1700)

HERE LIES MY WIFE
HERE LET HER LIE
NOW SHE'S AT REST
AND SO AM I

*   *   *

I told you I was ill.
– Epitaph of Spike Milligan

*   *   *

On the whole I'd rather be in Philadelphia.
– Epitaph of WC Fields (1880-1946)

*   *   *

Here Einstein lies,
At least, they laid his bier,
Just hereabouts or relatively near.

*   *   *

Lord she is thin. (Annapolis County graveyard)
A later carver has added an 'e' so it reads:
Lord she is thine.

*   *   *

Epitaph on a tombstone in a churchyard in Horsley
Down, Cumberland, erected to the memory of 'Mary,
wife of Thomas Bond' by her brother in law:

She was proud, peevish and passionate …
Her behaviour was discreet towards strangers;

But, imprudent in her family.

She was a professed enemy to flattery,

And was seldom known to praise or commend.

The talents in which she principally excelled,

Were difference of opinion, and discovering

Flaws and imperfections …

She sometimes made her husband happy with her good qualities;

But much more frequently miserable – with her many failings;

Inasmuch that, in 30 years' cohabitation he…

Had not, in the whole, enjoyed two years of matrimonial comfort.

At length,

Finding that she had lost the affections of her husband,

As well as the regard of her neighbours,

Family disputes having been divulged by servants,

She died of vexation, July 20, 1768

Aged 48 years.

* * *

Excuse my dust. This one's on me.
– Suggested epitaph of Dorothy Parker (1893-1967)

* * *

On the death of Matthew Arnold, Robert Louis Stevenson (1850-1894) wrote: "Poor Matt. He's gone to Heaven no doubt. But he won't like God."

*　　*　　*

Here lie I, Martin Elginbrodde.
Ha' mercy o' my soul, Lord Godde,
As I would do were I Lord Godde,
And thou wert Martin Elginbrodde.
– Anonymous

*　　*　　*

Here lies Fred
Who was alive and is dead:
Had it been his father,
I had much rather;
Had it been his brother,
Still better than another;
Had it been his sister,
No one would have missed her;
Had it been the whole generation,
Still better for the nation:
But since 'tis only Fred,
Who was alive and is dead –
There's no more to be said.

– Anonymous, quoted by Horace Walpole on Frederick,
Prince of Wales and House of Hanover, 1751.

*　　*　　*

Here lies John Tyrwitt
A learned divine;
He died in a fit
Through drinking port wine.
(Died 3 April, 1828, aged 59.)

*   *   *

Here lies cyclist Betty White
Who put out her left hand
And turned to the right.

*   *   *

Here lie I and my four daughters,
Killed by drinking Cheltenham waters.
Had we but stuck to Epsom salts,
We wouldn't have been in these here vaults.

*   *   *

An epitaph of a soldier who died of fever, contracted by drinking small beer when hot:

Here lies in peace a Hampshire Grenadier,
Who caught his death by drinking cold small Beer.
Soldiers be wise from his untimely fall,
And when you're hot drink strong or none at all.

*   *   *

And then this couplet:

> An honest soldier never is forgot,
> Whether he died by musket or by Pot.

*   *   *

If I had known it would come to this,
I would have come prepared.
— Poet David Thomas

10. SIGNS AND WONDER

The preacher for next week will be found hanging in the porch.

* * *

Men and women wanted to form congregation – no experience necessary.

* * *

Sign on the front door of a church undergoing extensive repairs: 'This is the Gate to Paradise' (will all visitors please go round and use the back entrance).

* * *

Sign outside a church in Cardiff: 'Last services before the motorway.'

* * *

The lesson next Sunday will be the 20th Chapter of Exodus – The Ten Commandments. You've seen the film – now come and hear the book.

*　*　*

A parked car had this text on the back window: 'Trust in the Lord.' Underneath, it said, 'This car is fitted with a crook lock.'

*　*　*

It is important in today's media age to get the sign outside the church building right. Vicar Joe has short-listed the following:

"Looking for a sign from God? This is it."

"No God – no peace. Know God – know peace."

"Free trip to Heaven. Details inside!"

"Searching for a new look? Have your faith lifted here!"

"Have trouble sleeping? We have sermons – come and hear one!"

Or maybe a picture of two hands holding stone tablets on which the Ten Commandments are inscribed and a headline thread that reads: "For fast, fast, fast relief, take two tablets."

*　*　*

A theological college held a special philosophy week. They produced colourful posters which contained just the one word: 'Think'. Wherever you went on campus, there were posters saying 'Think'. They were on the walls, in the canteen, lecture rooms and along the corridor. Someone stuck a poster in the gentleman's cloakroom. Above the washbasin it said, 'Think'. A student came along and with a felt pen, drew an arrow pointing towards the receptacle for soap, and wrote 'Thoap'.

*　　*　　*

A vicar decided to put up advertising signs outside his church. His first offering read: "If you are tired of sin, please step inside." The next day, he was horrified to see that someone had written underneath: "But if not, please telephone me on 295916."

11. BIBLE FACTS THAT MAY HAVE ESCAPED YOU

WHAT YOU MIGHT NOT HAVE KNOWN ABOUT SOME BIBLE CHARACTERS:

Adam – inventor of the loose-leaf system.

Ariel – patron saint of TV.

Delilah – ran earliest men's hairdressing salons; inventor of the 'short back and sides'.

Eve – first woman to persuade her husband to turn over a new leaf.

Goliath – a big man, with no head for drinks. David gave him a small shot and he got stoned.

Ham – son of Noah. Was in charge of the canteen on the ark. Patron saint of actors.

Levi – inventor of jeans.

Peter – first cricketer. He stood up with the eleven and was bold.

Moses – first tennis player. Scored in the Courts of the Pharaoh.

Soldier who slept on his watch – the smallest man in the Bible.

Woman of Samaria (Some-Area) – largest woman in the Bible.

U812 – phone number of the Garden of Eden (You Ate One Too).

Salome – danced naked in front of Harrods.

Samson – Early strong-man act. At one gig he brought the house down.

TOP TEN COMPLAINTS FROM BIBLICAL WOMEN:

10 Eve to Adam: You never take me anywhere different to eat!

9   Sarah To Abraham: Maybe if you stopped treating me like your sister, we could start a family! (Gen. 12:19)

8   Elizabeth to John the Baptist: I cook you a nice meal and all you want is locust, locust, locust!

7   Pharaoh's daughter to Moses: Stop parting the bath water, Moses, and wash behind those ears!

6   David's mum to Jesse, her husband: Do you really think it was a good idea to get David that sling? He's going to put someone's eye out!

5   Menorah's wife to her son Samson: Can't you clean the sink after you shampoo? I'm sick of all those long hairs!

4   Elizabeth to Mary: I love talking to you, Mary, I really do, but can you speak a little softer? This kid just won't stop doing the rumba in my tummy!

3   Mary to Joseph: I TOLD you to make reservations!

2   Herodias to her daughter: I told Herod that if he didn't do something about this John nut, I was sure the problem would come to a head!

1   Pilate's wife to Pilate after the resurrection: You never listen to me, do you? How do you feel now, Mr Wash-Your-Hands-In-Public? (Matt. 27:19)

*   *   *

The Ark has been delayed for 24 hours due to a spell of good weather. Mr and Mrs Noah are checking the animals:

Mr Noah: Elephants?
Mrs Noah: Two
Mr Noah: Camels?
Mrs Noah: Two
Mr Noah: Sheep?
Mrs Noah: Two
Mr Noah: Rabbits?
Mrs Noah: 197

*   *   *

As Moses came down the mountain, he said: "God has given me forty commandments." As he was speaking he slipped and fell badly. "Oops, that's ten."

WHY THERE ARE TEN COMMANDMENTS

OOPS!

* * *

"Does anyone know anything about the Phoenicians?"
"Didn't they invent blinds?"

* * *

When Adam wanted some sugar, he raised Cain.

* * *

There are two ice cream companies in the Bible – Lyons of Judah and Walls of Jericho.

* * *

What kind of lighting did Noah have in the Ark? Floodlights.

* * *

THE PRODIGAL SON – IN THE KEY OF F

Feeling footloose and frisky a feather-brained fellow forced his fond father to fork over the family finances.

He flew far to foreign fields and frittered his fortune feasting fabulously with faithless friends. Finally facing famine and fleeced by his fellows in folly, he found himself a feed-flinger in a filthy farmyard.

Fairly famished he fain would have filled his frame with foraged foods of the fodder fragments left by the filthy farmyard creatures. "Fooey", he said, "My father's flunkies are far fancier," the frazzled fugitive found feverishly, frankly facing facts.

Falling at his father's feet, he floundered forlornly.

"Father, I have flunked and fruitlessly forfeited family favour." But the faithful father, forestalling further flinching, frantically flagged the flunkies. "Fetch forth the finest fatling and fix a feast."

But the fugitive's fault-finding frater frowned on the fickle forgiveness of the former folderol. His fury flashed. But fussing was futile, for the far-sighted father figured: "Such filial fidelity is fine, but what forbids fervent festivity? The fugitive is found. Unfurl the flags, with fanfares flaring, let fun and frolic freely flow. Former failure is forgotten, folly forsaken, forgiveness forms the foundation of future fortitude."

ACKNOWLEDGEMENTS

My Lords, Ladies and Gentlemen … Reverend Sirs – Don Lewis (Celtic Publications, 1966)

Best Religious Jokes – compiled by Edward Philips (Wolfe Publishing, 1969)

Grave Humour – Fritz Spiegel

The Complete Book of Insults – Nancy McPhee (Published by BCA by arrangement with Andre Deutsh Ltd, 1995)

I Say, I Say, I Say – Brian Johnson (Methuen, 1994)

Father Douglas – J Derbyshire

Bill Balmforth
Peter and Jean Griffiths
Rona Campbell

Also available from Y Lolfa:

£9.95

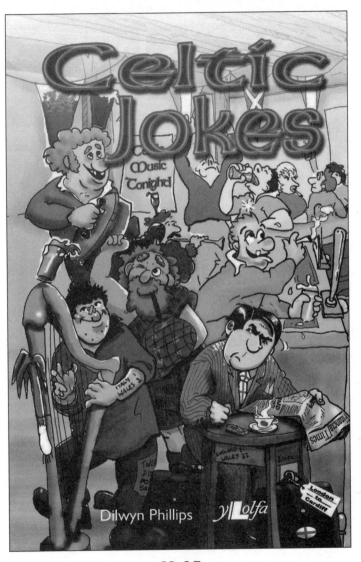

£3.95

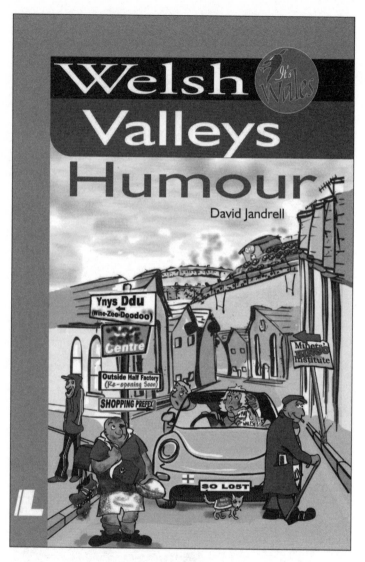

£3.95

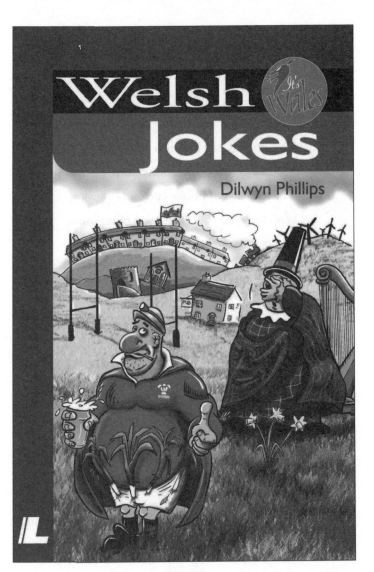

Welsh Jokes

It's Wales

Dilwyn Phillips

£3.95

This book is just one of a whole range of
Welsh interest publications from Y Lolfa.
For a full list of books currently in print,
send now for your free copy of our new,
full-colour Catalogue – or simply surf into
our website

www.ylolfa.com

for secure, on-line ordering.

Talybont, Ceredigion, Cymru SY24 5HE
e-*bost* ylolfa@ylolfa.com
gwefan www.ylolfa.com
ffôn (01970) 832 304
ffacs 832 782